Exercises in the Abstract:
Poems With No Name

Ty Gardner

Copyright © 2021 by Ty Gardner

Cover art copyright © 2021 by Shelly Gardner

All rights reserved. No part of this publication may be reproduced, stored in a retrieval system, or transmitted in any form or by any means, electronic, mechanical, photocopying, recording, or otherwise without written permission of the copyright owner except for the use of quotations in a book review.

For more information, address: gardnty@gmail.com

ISBN: 9798737091835

My sons,

    that you might know my heart, I gift you these nameless poems. Call upon me in these pages in your hour of need.

    —Dad

The tolling bells have long been rung,
and it seems I've missed the starting gun.

My memories of youth and love are wind-swept
and well behind me now,

               and what recollections left of boozing

beautiful women

    with bad habits

have all but washed away my good intentions.

Too many thoughts today.

A parade of quiet things I'd kept from myself have come back to celebrate; fear and shame and all the others with a name.

All the pretty floats and passers-by,
the ornate things
                that glisten

and blind the eye—reminders I was not enough.

Who'd've thunk this thing a waiting game?

Waiting to live, holding our breath and hoping for good news.

Waiting on the hands of time to come

back 'round and help us into an early grave.

But I can't afford to wait any longer.

It's time to run, time to run out of breath.

Bespill and deliver your graceless heart from the widdershins and wiles of a restless youth.

Let loose and cast out those beasts of

        bygones and dance contented,

                a repreival of regrets and shouldered-devil drudgery.

Bespill and deliver yourself of yesterday's trespasses.

There's blood on words I speak today,
and the messenger is no more.

I've killed to say the things I say.

    Sold my soul to the devil at midnight crossroads.

There'll be no reverie in death for me;
I'm in it for the long haul.

So love me in inked-pages my dears',
before my debt is due.

By summer's end,

on the eve of autumn's dawn,

            against the silhouettes of tented-pines along the
                                Blackfoot of Missoula,

lay me down with my brother and sisters

                    async the mooring stones of rivers smoothed,

and wash my hands and soul of soil and shame

                              that I might perceive glory.

5 a.m. has a feeling.
      A mood, like a song lyric you can't shake.

Has a taste,
      sharp as a pinch of the peppered salt flats beyond the Great Salt Lake.

It's a fixation, 5 a.m.,
      a venue where the possessed lie awake and obsess the little things:

particles,

moods,

lyrics.

At last,

of the bosom and breadth of the earth
do I remit my borrowed bones.

The burden of hymnal-feet upon the wallowing in lands of brush and dust are the stories not of my father's fathers',

but mine own, for I am a patron,

                weary,

                            of the days of Moses and his kin.

Sounds like that ol' winds at it again.

Stewin' and brewin' up something sinister.

Howlin' and prowlin' 'round like the night things that go bump.

Sounds like Hell out there.

Sounds like Hell in here.

Hell's what you make it, I s'pose.

Hell do I know? That's my mantra.

Quite a ruse, this haiku life;

to live and die in syllables of five/seven/five.

What more to say in such a space,
what mark to leave behind to change the world?

Did I write them all,
the words needed to better the hearts left in my wake?

I wonder in seaside reflections.

The regular things:

    football, church, and chicken dinners,

they don't satisfy me anymore.

I don't take solace in the traditional, in talking with God and upholding the doctrine of men.

        I find my truth in soaring free,
    high above the white noise of voices that would shout me

d

o

w

n.

Took some time, down 66,
to let the wind whisper wiles of desert dangers on blacktop miles.

To perch among the flowers wild,
as told by maidens of fire mane.

Took some time to leave behind the material, to get lost and left to my own devices.

To muse with sand and stone.

Tonight I dream a dandelion death.

A silent film storied in sepia overlay against a meadowed-backdrop where the convictions carried in my scattered spores idly glide in lands unknown.

Aloft to kindred minds who breathe in dust of poetic tomes and are contented by words.

Let the clouds alone, love.

Theirs is a life spent chasing moments,
pressed for time,
                and always pushing forward.

Best not to bother them with dreams, love;
nomads have no concern for the virtue of childish pastimes.

Theirs is a pursuit of dissipation, of lives like ours.

Who is this man with crooking nose, thin skin, and aching bones?
Does he know himself now in his children's laughter?
In their thumping hearts the same as his?
Can he catch his breath that the trivial desires of youth are faded?
Long retired and silly, who is this man?

Crawled in from the brick end of a broke down Brooklyn borough, a bookworm with a bum leg hopin' to borrow a buck.

Real existential type, sole black as the bottom of a beggar's boot, he was.

Sold his for a bottle of booze and a button-down, he'd said.

Helluva thing, that.

Let the cool of evening's blush draw over and coat the ember scribblings of a midday sun's erratic musings, like a cloak of ink and shadow to mask the sweltered-grief of sidewalks and city streets. Wordsmen crave to amble in melancholy there and wax poetic.

I've a theory,
      taut as strings that tug at the heart,
            that distance and stars

and road maps back to all your best memories,

the packed-back kind through distant special places unknown,

      rainstorm romances in parades of Ponderosa pines,

live on in words,

      eternal as time.

It seems, somehow,

the seagulls know a thing I don't.

Occurs to me they've seen the fragile cracks in the continuum,
know just when to

                swoop and swerve

                      to avoid being frozen in the source code.

A silent snicker at the thought;

maybe best not to let the normals in on it.

You've a voice I know and've heard before.

It comes to me in hushed tones from buried mementos—
memoried-graves of yesterdays.

Smiles a velvet simile of love like death,
of menacing metaphors to remind that one is not fulfilled
without the other.

To lay claim my soul, it speaks.

It would've been the could've beens',

I can say that much for sure.

All the things that should've been,

moonlight marauders taking off

and making out with a trove of all the treasured tales of love,

caching them like candy.

Souls aflame a sunset blushed,

we would've been.

Blacktop sunrise on the highway of my parting;

desert mornings are deserted here,

and there's no one left to pass.

A final blinker down memory lane—pictures and parcels of poems from life on the road throughout my road of life.

Nowhere left but onward now,

into eve's dusk.

A maddening world we're living in;

wrong is right, up is down.

Takes restraint to keep the tongue tied to the roof of your mouth.

Requires time to kill with kindness, each word a stranglehold.

Means doing more,
putting on your Sunday best to beat Monday kind of madness.

Sometimes,
> I don't write a thing;
a thing writes me.

I don't always mean what I say,
> but I always say what I mean.

Sometimes,
> I'm the pen,
ink-teeming and spilling.

I'm sooty blots of Rorschach mess that split and bleed off the page.

That drain away and dry,
> sometimes.

Makes you wonder about people, the coming and going.

Where they've been, and where they're headed.

Makes me wonder at the rag-clad man pushing around his life's achievements in a shopping cart—my sisters', who've abandoned their innocence for amusement,

makes no sense.

Had they only warned me of the melancholia in
the reddening of autumn's leaves,
the sadness of the sun,

sobered an ashen-flax by the dispatching of summers' squandered in
reckless youth.

The despair we come to know in naked lands of winter's ire; had they
only warned me.

Sweet,
       aye, bitter as sweet,

bitter as budding fruit,
     low,
lo o'er bristled-fields scorched, scoured raw of the heat of an unforgiving God on high,

   high lord of a godless coterie,

              sycophants of death,

alive without ever living,

            unable to change,

to risk love,

             to permute.

Oh,

that I could have said them one last time, friend.

Weighted words oft wasted in momentary exchanges.

What depths of sacrifice would I endure now
to know the song in your heart on days like this?

To indulge a verse and sing with you?

The cruelty of time, I lament, is wisdom.

I loathe the way I push and pull;

I'm ocean waves in thunderstorms that clash electric and cuff the prows of simple ships with thrashing hands of bittered-squalls.

I'm pained by the disappointment in becoming a spectator of memories abandoned, writing,

    and loathing

always...

A moment now to jot it all down;
tell it my way, narrate it as I remember it.

Between the fuzz of weekday benders,
I'll make amends for becoming my father.

Maybe.

Or maybe I'll piss away my pension and hate myself.
Laugh when I'm drunk,

and be somber whenever I'm sober.

Beyond the beyond,

just afore the vaulted gates of Etherea

where I receive the omega and ascend to reconcile my earthly trespasses that I might accompany kith and kin in graced-lands of pined-repose,

a moment of truth to salve
        or shatter
all hope—the hour of redemption.

In marrowed-field of bone and blood,

a sapling Spruce with needles red stood alone amidst the dead.

Its roots knew strength from the flesh of men,
and with time

        grew tall and wide.

That barren field a place of quiet happiness now where I sit with the lone   Spruce and listen to the past.

Of ocean sands in seaside sunsets,
I'd come to know the truth of the planes of this world and the next.

It came as no surprise,
unsettling as the harshness of shadowed-wings

swooping low above the effervescence,
beating to the drum of death: there is no love, no light.

I ponder at the things I've penned,

                                                                        now and again,

and wonder at the words,

                                                  where they've wandered,

and the kinds of conversations conceived of their constitution.

Will they still say my name a hundred years from now?

                                                              A thousand?

Drives me barking mad with curious desire.

Were that I so much more for the ones I love.

That simple things,

gestures in words,

were enough;

that I could give my skin and bones and heart in transitive prose that transformed

and touched the wild spirit of the wascally—the wabbit ones,

lovely and weary of wilting.

A song,

lyrics unsung,

on a soundtrack to your life.

A chorus there, palpable as Angels' aflight the impregnable sky;

something akin to a composition of cloud-crescendoed chaos

where violence and vitriol collide in a cavalcade of nuance.

A psalm there,

to play you out.

I did not cry for the dead.
I remember that.

I wept instead
for the dying,

for unspoken words that amaze
but never stood a chance,
       and all the unanswered amens.

For the careful hands that dressed those bodies draped
in nature's cloth,
and deliverance from troubled limbs,

I wept.

Never planned a stone slow death;

didn't mean for the head and the heart
to hurt each other that way over feelings.

Would've never even dreamed division of this kind.

Like speckled-mot particles in sunshined-window's dusk,

I'm gradually gravitating towards dusting-sill.

Another day, another turn.

Another rotation 'round this fishbowl existence.

I've lived here before, and I'll do it once more.

It's circular, you know?

A cycle.

We'll come back,

again and again,

until we realize there is no value in routine,

no purpose in perfect linens.

I recall a rural Americana youth.

Portraits of hardened men on horseback graced the walls of my grandmother's woodland home,

and the currency of cheap backtalk came at the high cost of smarted-cheeks.

Stiff lips and pistoled hips were a mark of strength—an incentive.

Coursing-grays have settled where flaxen filament once swooped and fell over the coupled bead of emeralds enlivened.

A winter's spring has summered into eternal fall, and I am haunted by the fearlessness of seasons in the shadow of the reaper, tormented by my mortality.

It was a "take care" type of goodbye.
The kind that hopes for something more,
    an invitation, like slender fingers that slide across an open
door, pleading eyes and pressed lips
        too shy to say please.

Sometimes, though,
    sorry is better suited,

and it's better to deny.

Fancy me, a satellite,

doting and adoring earth's loving tones of chroma, absorbed by the atmosphere and pulled into its aura.

And when the twinkly things flitter-flash and fade,

play me out a prelude—little overtures of ocean operas and notes harmonic in star symphonics.

Morning dawn stretches east to west,

and somewhere in the still dark,

there is light—a fusion of skin and sweat in thrash and thrum.

There are life and longing,

and a simple understanding in the silence—misplaced love

found again in the moments before the sun's cresting.

A daring thing to die weightless; to dismiss your deepest fears and sigh away your sins. To mantle your heavy heart and climb into eventide's carriage, up and away to skylines celestial. Who among us knows a clear conscious in earthly reflection, I ask?

I sigh and ask.

Everything's a slow burn now—slow love,
lovemaking; slow to come, slow to go.

Slow dance, slow down, and slower yourself to hers.

Slow pulse, slow rise, slow fall to a slow rhythm.

Nothing's random anymore,
                        positions with purpose.

The pretense to the pace is
                        palpable.

Hit me good and hard at thirty-three,
a damnable dread I'd eventually come to treasure.

Fought it long as I could before that,
      the truth of things,
           but thirty-three was a great time to call it quits,
         and the dread settled in.

We mind each other now,
                that old dread and I.

There's no one more alone than you,

                    than me,

                                      than us.

I've been the anything,

          the (in-between),

the everything.

You've been the distance,
        the expanse,

all the little things I write about.

We've been day and night at different times,
and there's no one more alone than us.

Eight years have aged my folks,

guess it's been a while since I've been home.

Guess they'd say the same, though, but maybe that's just the six a.m. silence speaking.

Perhaps I'm putting off the portent things,

peacemaking with the past and present.

Guess it's been a while.

When it's curtains, dear; when cast and crew have all come to call me home,

keep us close in calming eyes and tender hand.

In cheek-to-cheek affection.

In steady breath and simple tongue.

In longing gaze of love's adjourn,
        until embraced of divine return,
keep us close.

Nothing hurts the way it did before—shoulders,
bones and broken hearts.

It's in our nature to be this way.
Aches and pains act up a little more at this age,

and getting older is feeling all the things,
even if you don't want to.

Seventeen and softer skin was another time,

and the snooze is going off again.

I know the heft of caskets and

the weight on wet cheeks at funerals.

The value of vocabulary in eulogies that praise the departed

and the laboring silence that suffocates the space between the empty seats of a vehicle on the drive home.

                                                              I know and drive.

All I do is write. A letter here, a syllable there.

Little beaded things threaded onto sentence strings.

                        But when it's time,
                        I won't scrawl a word,

                                not a single line: no anecdotes or clever notes,

no literary alliterations, no reason, no rhyme.

I deserve to fade quietly.

The good days are an abomination at best.

Giving a mile and getting an inch in return—5,280 steps closer to being 6 feet under.

The bad days are a blizzard,
like the taste of television static on your tongue.

Everything else between is just that:

space for every
                      thing.

Sog and mudded-brine crimped the scents of salty air in towns all along the western coast.

We'd paused a pinch for a golden pint or three in musking-dives

and stole a kiss between bluegrass folktales.

The weathered wooden floors creaked in slow dance courtship as we sway.

Four more laps to go. 5 a.m., and I'm on the run,

out of breath and far behind, far from finishing,

from the finish line, from the grand finale.

So much for being steadfast.

For staying stalwart.

For showing up when it counts.

It's 5 a.m. with four laps, and I'm on the run.

Glass folks are tempered wrong;
you see it in the hairlines—finite fractiles that bend the light
               and boast colors broad and beautiful to behold.

But glass folks need a steady hand to tend their fragile hearts.
            One crack can change everything,

and they're never the same.

And so it came to pass,

we'd laid a good friend down in the January sun,

snow-hidden hibiscus asleep in spring-lingered slumber.

He'd made a sacrifice at seventeen,

the hard kind you can't walk away from,

and I've not been back in many a spring;

I wonder of hibiscus.

That ol' outbound train is shovin' off soon,

rickety-tickin' 'cross the countryside on steel beams,
and coal shoveled steam.

A wink and a wave from the back end of a boxcar will
have to suffice, love.

I'm runnin' behind outrunnin' the horizon and tryin' to outlast livin'.

My poet mouth gets me into trouble;

                what can I say?

I've traded good looks for a silver tongue,

        and I'm amusing when I'm brooding over my muses.

When I'm penning my pissy mood over lost lovers in the layered obscurity of my poems—I prefer to talk it out by typewriter.

Inspired.

    I recall that foremost.

        The words were unique,

            dazzling like diamonds in the lamplight,

                radiant as star shine on moonless nights;

                    the sentences were sugar-sweet and dripped

                        a candy glaze right off the page.

But time hardens all things and burdens brittle love.

The moon and me, we're a problem, sea?

I'm ebb and flow, she's come and go,
my tides they rise by her decree.

But push or shove, it's cosmic love;
she's hallow beams from skies above.

I'm salt and splash in wind and thrash,
her moods do get the best of me.

Problems, sea?

Rims of white wines lipped-red and peppered glass
on cheap linoleum.

Echos of oak and fist and irritability over the in-laws—
little things we won't remember till the mid-morning grog.

It started the usual way,

over an ornament,

and ended with dead silence

and a dustpan.

I don't care to be a dad today, not the way storm clouds slap the Savannah threshes in June.

Not the way cyclic things do what they do because they don't know better—the way it's in their nature.

Today's a day of being a hurricane,

swirling rage and spit, not a dad day.

We'd weathered storms and looked to God;

wondered about the quiet,
questioned how someone could be so silent.

And still the storms.

Always the storms.

We cried in commas,

little pauses to catch our breath before the run-on rains.

And still the storms.

Always the storms.

You want to talk poetry?
Let's talk in tongues.

Let's tie each other up in twisted thoughts
that titillate our touchy things.

Let's speak about sensuality in the shadow of seven different
languages and dive into each other's dialects.

You want to talk?
Yammer me good.

I may not write a thing today; the words are lost, can't find a way.
I may not say a thing at all, my mind encased of winter's shawl.

I've not a sentence to aspire, from penning thoughts I shall retire.
Come 'round again on the morrow; I might've worked out all my sorrow.

Life's all firsts up to a point.

        First breaths,

        first words.

      First kiss, first love, first heartbreak.

First sunrises that set on the first day you'll never see someone again—true first's firsts.

Life's all firsts up to a point,
        and it's very rare to ever be happy after.

Deepest regret,
twenty years strong,
alive and well in song lyrics and certain film scenes,
is the life I didn't save,
the one that counted on a phone call to make the difference.

Januarys' get a little colder each year just in case I forget;
twenty strong, my regret.

Whatever it could have been, it was,
and I'm too tired now to make it work.

1985 was the last year of true love for this old ghost,
and the time to give up the grave has finally come.

No half-truths.

No more lies, just a courtesy to 1985 and the last year of true love.

It's the rough-and-tumble tussle,
the hard-knock body bustle that makes me beg.

The gag and grapple bump-and-grind,
the lug-and-tug me from behind that makes her plead.

The rip and roar of crashing shores,
the blast of salt on harbor ports that make us beg for mercy.

It was the small hours,
      my cousin and I pushing around his Matchbox mobiles,
pretend playing we ran the city,
      desperados living out our wildest dreams.

But then a beast, his stepfather,
      very real and not imaginary,
burst in and beat his head against the bed stand as the
townspeople looked on in terror.

Stripped off our society skin and jumped,

bone naked and without inhibition,

into the blue beyond and welcomed the crush of ocean hands.

Daylight and the dread of fresh air were at our backs,

and we drove deeper to live our lives anew in the wide wonder of coral gardens.

To set your flesh aflame with pleasure, a burn that burrows

nerve deep and boils the bloodstream.

To watch you wax and wane and wiggle

in silk sheet seas that wrap things up and bring you to the point

in the silence of Sunday morning euphoria—the simple stuff I think on.

Travelers, we; nomads called to nowhere lands,

hearkened to the heights of the Sierras where sugar pines shake hands with the clouds—destined for desert air through our palms and the brush of ocean salt in our hair.

Travelers, we,

searching for release in simple things.

Spirits overflowed, and cold souls were warm once more.

A pinch of blood, and Mary,

and a dash of the good Dr.'s bootlegged bourbon,

set a curved line where once snow-cold and salted scowls perched as birds of midnight black.

Pellets of crystalline crashed down outside.

Fourteen was a fog that I've thought to forget,

and it's strange to wonder where twenty-odd years went.

Misted-mornings, when the sun is lost, feels like fourteen,
                                          and I pine for cracks and
sinking sockets.

For peace in aging, far and away from fourteen's fog—from despair.

No funeral for me, thanks.

No farewell or fanfare to see me out of this infernal festival of flagrant foolishness.

A few friends, the wilting flower types with words for bones,
to say a thing or two;
        to scatter my ashes in winds of sonnets and psalms.

No funeral for me.

Slurred speech and forgetfulness weren't even the worst I'd seen of him.

Sticky hardtops and stitches,

        bruised brow lines from bad falls,

                and those shrunken eye sockets weren't either.

It was the stink of it, deep in the pores when he'd sweat that I knew his affliction.

Nothing's getting said tonight.

There's promise in the blush of silent eyes that stare and search their lover's gaze—like practiced lips that know.

Everything's telepathy when you're tangled like a telephone cord, twisted like a serpent with a lust to be their servant.

Could've walked with Angels if I'd wanted.

Chose,
to tango with the Devil on a daisy dream dance floor instead.

One snap of the wrist and the place was vacant,

barren, and boring as cupboards when shadows scatter
and vacate the light—chose to exorcise my demons in dance.

Haunted by vermillion smiles, I'm hunted and hunting in dreams of pre-dawn woods.

I've a scent of something I lost, just ahead, just behind,

all around, side to side—demons closing in to collar and carry me off into the darkness.

I steady my pen to write away all my sins.

Lucky in love, or no luck at all;

love's been a turnstile that way.

                People coming,

                                  people going,

        sunrise easts that settle west,

                              but I'm never lonely.

I learned how to be alone early,

so I'm used to ghosts at dusk and incessant floorboards that refuse

                                  to quietly settle.

Perfect is as perfect does—a perception of the pieces for some, a romantic notion for others.

But where there's a stuffed pipe of smoked stigmas, there's fire,

        Soaring,

   I'm

and

sky-high in clouds of my shame.

Always the shame.

Startled by a sensation of falling,

I wake.

Good morrow
>bones, ache, and jaded skin.

Good morning
>fire, and smoke, and burned down house.

Good morning
>balding, fat, and middle age.

Good day
>dark, and clouds, and overcast.

Good to see you, gas prices.

Good morning to everything and everyone but the one who made my heart cold.

How to write a thing today, with wind and snow conspiring against the sun just beyond my terrace door.

What to say when the cold and cunning of December drear have whited over my canvas of words?

A scream into the deafening void,

    perhaps,

beating and bruising my chest?

They say to consult a spirit if you're curious about valor;

to hug a headstone if you're ready to die and too scared to do it.

I say petition a poet for a poem of parables that draw parallels between a life wasted and wasting away in a grave— paradoxes of the pointless.

I thought about the west today, the old one you see in filmstrips and fuzzy photos—black and whites of outlaws and outcast types.

I liked that people didn't smile back then.

They didn't know any better, maybe.

Didn't know how I s'pect.

Either way, I liked it, the old west.

The burdening hour again.

Somewhere between reluctant eyes and restlessness,

I'm at it.

Babbling in the shaded hours about a poetess, wandering the neon haze of abandoned city streets with a high-grade heat rash on my heart—fevers from a love-fervor wrong I can't right off.

It's taxing,

and I'm tired.

Maybe as stones,

we'd have known each other better—weather-smoothed versions of ourselves condemned to the cool of lake bottoms by boyish hands.

Had we only skimmed the glass surface of still waters once more on our voyage into the

unknown,

        maybe

we'd have had a chance.

Lord knows I've done my best, it's 5 a.m.,
and I'm in a mood again.

Turning on every light to watch the shadowed things
scurry and scatter,
hoping to have no hard feelings today,
        hoping to hang out the hang-ups and air 'em out.

To overturn my terrors,
        Lord knows I've tried.

The words today are like indolent fish.

I tempt them with my laden quill, a feathered thing ornate with gilded-thatch,
       but they quickly curtail the chase.

These parchment waters are warm,
       and the lines cannot be swayed to surface—
       the words are   shy,

       indolent, as lazy fish.

Idol hands that course and quest
the generous landscape of your divine form;
you're my weekend getaway, I'm your midnight shower scene.

It's fifth-gear-freeway fogged windshields and whispered perversions
when we're together, the way nothing matters to a nihilist.

Back then,

    it wasn't me that would jump from the edge;

it was the edge that would jump from me—something about britches,

        two sizes too big and the whole of the world inside my palm.

Time and tide took me down a size,

and here I stand,
    praying to God I can f l y.

The room was spinning cheap champagne,
and something alternative
        (late '93 maybe?)
hung a low bassline heft from the ceiling like crepe paper streamers.

We danced our blues out in glasses midnight black wearing nothing but our briefs and watched the streamers wilt away.

Hard rain; the kind that builds up near city sidewalks and gets whiplashed by passing cars.

We knew the danger of a love like hard rain but pulled

our ponchos up and over our back and brow just the same.

Tough times hailed down in sheets of sleet,

and still, we walked.

I'm a cluster of all the things that make me tick;

the overgrowth of grass in suburban lawns,

the irritability of overdressed grocery shoppers.

The obnoxiousness of flaunted opulence

and the awkwardness of a missing Oxford—I'm a gaggle of the things that get me going.

Better you than me, better us than we.
Best to go than stay; better's better off that way.

Better's best when playing nice—better's better paradise.
Better bet we'll be our best, better than you would've guessed.

Best be going, better gone, best part of a love hurt song.

I need the taste of salt on my tongue, the tang of your temple on my tastebuds as I take you to paradise.

I want the goosebumping
                        from face thumping

and the smack and smart
                        of my favored flavor of flesh.

I long for the ache of being winded—
the begging of bated breathing.

I know my blood a bond in ocean spittle.

This once solid crustacean husk now merely a suit of dough and filling long for the baker's oven.

Evolution has been unkind to the spawn of our sporozoan ancestors, and,

little
       by
              little,

we slowly convenience ourselves to death.

Midnight in the middle of Texas thunderstorms.
There were croaking things that made a splash somewhere in the silence between intervals of lightning strikes.

I lie in the swamp and soak of crabgrass,

twirling an already dead flower in my fingers,

contemplating its disease.

Some days are just big sad without any ado.

So much to say,

but no bottled ink to wet your pen—best save it for tomorrow when the sun's out again.

Some days your comforter's the only comfort you take,

the way it blankets

and pulls you

back

into the depths of your dissonance.

Perhaps it's the predator inside me,
an internal howling that beckons and begs the pursuit of skin-to-skin indulgence—little gratifications of the good things.

Perhaps it's the call of your wiles that keep me on the prowl and pawing through midnight woods for a carnal catharsis.

I sweat the salt of today's bitterness into my bathwater and fix a
scowl at hard water residue.

The tiles tell tales of someone else's residual resentment
despite the scald and scrub of harsh chemicals.

I hope for nothing now but reflect the things I should beware of.

Rise and shine,
rise and run; the city streets are calling.

Come slush or sun, the pavement is a perfect place to get away from the daily grind—the one between your plates and blades and the jawbone grit from clenched teeth.

Run to escape,

run to catch up,

rise and run.

I've sighed into bruised city air at one a.m. so hard I thought the sidewalks would swallow me whole to shut me up.

I've bullied a cigarette butt for blowing smoke up mine

and even accused the sun of hiding behind clouds on purpose.

Nothing's wrong,

but I'm not right.

Flirtations like a butterfly wing will do just fine—foolish infatuations in flight patterns that don't seem feasible.

Let there be bodies that
      bre ak
from their biology

and go
                    their own way,

like a sensuality that can only make sense to arcing backs and fluttering hearts.

Fifteen and a dope fiend, I think on that now and again.
Could've started long before, but who knows?

Poor kid was dead at birth, a long shot not long for this earth.

Overdosed at twenty-eight; heroin, I believe.

I excused myself from work for his funeral but never went.

Apartments where paper-thin walls resound the plight
of lovers' conquest;

where the smacking sounds of temperamental tongue talk seeps
through cheap sheetrock,

        and the stale of days-old seduction

                flavors cross threads of hundred count linens;

I'm known to pen my vices.

The last time we had lunch,

might've been that sixth street café,

    I should've known;

could've seen it coming if I'd paid attention.

All the bad times and boozin',

    I was cruisin' for a heartbreak bruisin'.

You were a lifeline then—a lighthouse for the lost,

    and I blew it.

Point taken.

Two points for putting me down on paper.

Props for penning yourself the protagonist.

High praise for presuming what's what and how we proceed now.

A pat on the back for pushing me away and convincing yourself I got the things I want—point made, point taken.

Better to know
no
   thing
about
any
   thing
than to know
every
   thing
about nothing?

No
   body

can replace the hurt from having nobody, over or under;
it all hurts the same.

Some
   thing

with someone else isn't necessarily something from my experience,

and
no
   one
      person will do.

Some kind of silent suffering I couldn't understand had taken over, and granddad was never the same after.

He was absent-minded at his best, and knew nothing at his worst.

I can still see gran crying when he couldn't remember her one morning, and I understand it now.

One more mood song today,

and I might just go from nothing to something—
I could just bubble over and burst.

Another lyric about love and I'll lose it;

drive up to the northern Florida pan,

and fly off the handle.

Sing me anything but the big sads;

I'm already in a mood.

Thinking back on things I wouldn't do again—little blunders bought and paid with youthful ignorance.

I wouldn't linger on a hug;

I'd lean in and give myself to someone first.

I wouldn't leave with "I love you" on my lips,

and I wouldn't smile through my grief.

I'd own it.

Every poem is someone's penance—bits of our bard parts that bleed atonement ink onto slips of sorrowed-stationary.

Each stanza speaks to the transgressions tucked within our damnable DNA, and the corruption we carry comes through in the successive lines of a couplet.

Summer's over too soon for my taste;

autumn asks my hand to dance amidst the scatter of loose leaves
to divert my attention before the cold and crush of winter's hug,

but I long for May's June evening kumbaya conversations
by the campfire.

Summer's over too soon for my taste.

Question my convictions, and you'll see I have none.

I know only what I've seen and heard,

what I observe one minute to the next,

what I feel in the slap of a rainstorm,

and the sensation of first-time lips.

Argue me a man without regard,

and I'll contend my contentment.

Dreamless sleeping can't be beat;

give me blank space with a pitch-black backdrop.

I can't sleep when I dream;

the toil of tilling all my sown sins under an eclipsed sun drives these trowel hands to a deep ache.

In the morning,
              I scrub the ash of clay soil from my hands.

Right there, in the splash of dramatic ocean salt and the violence of
a violet-red summer sundown,

I made a mental note of every wild strand,
the curve and crook of each indented cheek,

        what kindness carried in the cosmos of indigo-green irises,

to call on when I dream.

Goodbye got the better of me that day;
seventeen's too soon, friend.

People speak of sunshine at a funeral service,
                                      and I wonder what that's like.

Wonder what's the point of it all when February fumbles your
long-forgotten name—headstones are humorous that way,
                                                  I guess?

33 without purpose;
I remember penning my last
will and testament
beneath a pine tree reprieve from summer sizzle.

I can still feel the sting of salt on dry lips when I think on the tears
that sprang loose

and the thrum of a collapsing heart in my eardrums as I wrote.

December plates shift tectonic,

and I mourn the passing of another year.

The dog days are indeed over, as I've heard it said,

and I look to my sons to take up the tablet
and tell the story of their father,

a bitter man with little room in his heart,

not unlike his own.

A poet never truly dies, and that's a fact;

check it with your peers if I can't persuade you.

We're broken and bruised beings that live on in the afterlife of the lines we write—radical things with no rationale,

living only to be remembered.

What could be more rational?

Wish a dying man good luck and godspeed with a heartfelt hug.

Hand in hand, head to his,
and whisper your last "I love you."

Fluff a pillow or two for comfort,

then bunk him in with his favorite blanket and don't bother with the breathing—the hardest part is halfway over.

Speak my sentience in simple sentences; I've no more constitution of the human condition than the common houseplant.

                   I understand combustion,

    violent and volatile,
the process of energy transference,

movement that can neither be created nor destroyed—
we are merely carbon.

Someone's shooed away, the sunshine—another one gone,
pancreatic this time.

Another soul sent to live among the Polaroids,
another mantled-smile added.

I won't speak of forgiveness on February's behalf from here on out.

Even the months of the year must be held accountable.

Lichen trails have frosted oaken husk where once I stood in fescue fields among my beech brothers and spoke of sapling things.

Time and tension have rendered me hostage to retreating roots, and I find myself now in disbelief at the spaces between these dendrite rings.

You and I, we are the glass—half-full and full of ourselves,

full of it for the most part and unfulfilled for the other.

It's the arrogance that gets us.

We occupy the same space and speak volumes about the distance between us.

You and I, we are the glass—empty.

Alone.

I must've been my father's age when he told the tale
                    (a thing he seldom did cold sober)
of a time from his Idaho youth,

slowly reaching for a struggling pup just before it slipped beneath
the ice of a half-frozen river.

His midnight silhouette still haunts me even now.

Lord,

    lay me down in the bedrock of these creek bottoms and let the ease of the earth's Epsoms swell over and salt my jilted resolution. I've been in a faithless frame of mind for far longer than I can recall, and there's a steep price to living a life with no value.

Someone's first breath will be my last;

make no mistake, in a blink, I'll be atmosphere.

Comforts me to know I'll be energy—
the tingle you'll feel in the fine hairs on your arm when I pass through.

Puts me at ease to presume I'll have purpose outside this mortal shell.

Can we hop on the good foot and skip to the bad parts yet?

Jump past the point of no return and put our tainted deeds to task.

Smash our bones together and see what chemistry we make—
alchemists of love and lust;

everything in life's a mistake until you get it just right.

Even in a dream, there are things I can't recall.

That summer,

before the rose bush failed and I swore at the tartness
of my mother's rhubarb, perhaps?

Something foreign lingers low,

in the corner,

bursting as a shadow does in sunlight
when I get too close to remembering.

I've been too hard on sons I love,
        pushed to bend where curves won't fit,

                and pulled at strings with centers frayed.

I'm the furthest thing from finifugal, and in time I'll reap the labor of stale oats sown in the eyes of hardened men—I confess to being what I fear most.

Lakeside stroll and we're alone; frothy tides befriend and pool our careless footprints.

The silence of the still surface says more now
       about our situation than we ever could,
              and I wonder of life beyond the approaching outlet.

Is there anything around the corner for us?

Today I'll test myself at the pulpit and speak for the dead;

Lord knows I love the conflict of pressing eyes from the audience—
the demand to do right by the deceased and paint a portrait of a life in words.

The pressure to be an impressionist invigorates,

                                                   and I paint.

The coarse scratch of a ballpoint is lost on me—
I can't recall the sound.

I'm more familiar with the inhospitable feel of bathroom tile lately

than sensations of notepad scribblings; more in tune with the tempo of a thumping cranial capillary than the rhythm of a poem.

Not so much the bad taste as the habits;

I wander off to get lost,

but every foolhardy gambit begets a pity party—even the good gamblers are going to lose their ace hole now and again.

And like a good boy, every dog knows when to tuck his tail

    and shuffle home

ashamedly.

Once more,

and I won't feel fit to look myself in the mirror—night terrors will find the back door to my daydreams

and let themselves in if it happens again.

Another squandered chance to say goodbye before the part about

"rest in peace,"

and I'll forfeit my humanity.

Somewhere in a slow song,

                the barn door is shut.
                I choose to slap your mother's hand away,

      hold and take her wet cheeks to mine.

Tell her there's nothing in there for her and that random thoughts of rafters and rope will only haunt her.

The song ends. Did it ever start?

Snow like paper flakes salt the suburb terraces on my late-night slow drive,
and I wonder about a girl—a woman now,
                        I remind myself and muse my surprise.

I think to write a letter,
        people did that once I seem to recall, but a random streetlight flickers and dissuades me.

A quarter past your something or other,

when you napped the littles and broke the despair of the day down,

and all I did was listen, that's when we were real.

When we could shut the world out and seal ourselves into video screen smiles, that's when we were at our best.

Fidget hands with two left feet; I fumbled over to a '90s bass line, hoping we could dance.

The pickup line was shoddy,
      but we snickered about it later over something fruity—like a punchline in a spiked punch bowl;
                                we continued laughing.

A DJ that wouldn't last kept us going.

We read and muse the day's paper over early morning coffee.

Mow the lawns and birth our children, binge the things,

                    and buy the stuff.

We dream dreams and dress our best, do our hair,
and keep tradition.

We file taxes and fill in the forms and fade away—we muse

                    and

                    fade.

First time for last time's sake,
I can't seem to say the things you'd like me to.

It was half-truths or heartache
when December doled out an ultimatum,
and ultimately we favored the flavor of living like a lightning flash—
seems you did mean forever when we parted ways.

How to write about a heavy sigh, the kind that lives to breathe your name in the scramble of an afternoon impulse?

The very sort who would collude with stars and bring cosmo-crossed lovers' to life from dream.

How to pen the grief of love,

lost to the idea of an exhale?

Summer rains can't come soon enough—how they motivate the movement of seasons.

Winter windows are cool to the touch, but a deep pane lies within the frosted glass.

The wilt and will of weather tides left behind by waves of whiteout oceans, born to life anew in budding spring.

I think, perhaps, I'll not sit this wanting heart out any longer,

this leathered and bone-knocked thing that still skips a beat while rounding the bases.

I have a tendon, see,

        to bench my feelings and play it safe.

In time,

        I'll tend to my considerable garden of regrets.

Sunday slow cruise and sunglasses;

I didn't want to encourage bad behavior,

but coke bottles on cherry lips bring it out of me,

and I couldn't let insinuating smiles slip by.

Somewhere between a Mulholland glide down and ventures through Ventura, we pulled the top up.

Wherever those porcelain cheeks pillow down tonight,
I pray the kindness of someone's philanthropic palms,

someone to bear witness to the tearful testimony of my trespasses
and atone my tendered resignation as I should have.

    I say these things in the name of love,

        amen.

The departed will never talk about the deep plunge taken within themselves just before their death,
    but the dying will.

I've listened
    to whispers of pain and penitence

far into the haunt of midnight dark—little bedside secrets sighed into the black just before the black.

Hard plunge today; everything's got the better of me.

Little things,
the consistency of bread and kombucha pucker,
                                                  put me on edge.

Zoom schooling and the irritability of being questioned will surely put me six feet under.

Hard plunge and I'm holding up for a wine down.

I might ask to see the sun again, hard to say.

An hour of silence, maybe, or a conversation with my steel string;
find that rhythm again and get moody.

Perhaps I'll putter around the house like a ghost,

popping out from behind a half-hearted peek-a-boo,
but who can say?

Dean-cool how we can't contain ourselves;
two rebels with no regard,
without a cause and kite-high on ignorance.

My leather jacket baby, your blue jean bad boy,

we're a two-seater beater with a fresh coat and a tune-up—
Hell on wheels with no regard, without a cause.

Sold a banjo once to make rent;
a comely piece without a scratch,
nickel-plated on walnut finish, gifted to me by my father.

Now,

seldom have I hidden my eyes from another in shame,
but, friend,

I tell you this,
I've never hung my head so low when asked to pluck a tune.

Daughter of the highway plains,

    tonight I am the weathervane; a wayward thing susceptible to the slightest breeze, eager to dart away on western winds as far south as the light of the north star will take me before the eastern sunrise.

Tonight,

                I take flight. Away, away.

Nevada cacti know the favor of the desert sun,

the kindness of the mother moon and sister stars,

the bounty of the burrowed loam,

the company and conversations of the tiny cactus wren,

and a great many other afforded wisdoms the omnipotence of man has yet to discover.

Back,

>before the story of the noon-high sun and the salted brows of men;
>before clouds and their fleeting pretenses of silver linings,
>my Mother wept her ocean rains to satiate wilds abandoned.

But the sea, a damnable drunk,
sired the tides to whip and crash her shores.

Pine dusk patrons press in the folded hush of campfire burnout, sand, and sage to scent their morn tide movement.

I mull the idea of calling after them with a gentle 'tsk' on my teeth, but reason to let them mill about before they note my presence— we share the quietude.

By tender courtesy of evening lamp,
I quiver delightedly at the hollow of my ballpoint.

Whet with intrigue,

I splay the pastel incubus of my ink-mare poetry across the pressed spaces of blank—dactylic demons that spring from my pen;

the devil inside me is at it again.

Remember your father's hands,
the callused affection they've shown in times of need.

Remember your mother's mannered tongue, how she wore her
hardships with the grace of a ballroom gown.

Remember,
for the sake of remembering.

For the sake of saying your people were here.

Someday,
      on a Sunday,

when the linseed finish is just so,

and you've managed to fold back the final page of that secondhanded first edition,

when the last cuppa turmeric and cinnamon spice tea has touched down on your tongue,

let me loose on scattered winds
      and smile.

Took a dust scrub once underneath an oolong sun to oxidize and
smooth my shameful skin;

                a swoop of dusk-black and cawing creatures,

couriers of wasteland tidings, circled noncommittally as I bathe.

I dreamt of crimson and pale on lavender silk
and how you were never shy.

Error of my ways, we meet at last.

The Pinot moon is calling for a confession, and I'm inclined to abide.

I am moved to howl and manifest my trespasses
under cover of conifers.

To chorus,
      drunkenly,
kissing with close friends and castigating
the good word of the gospel.

It was shadows from the shade of Venetian shudders what made me
think of dreamers; how I've given and received love from them.

A ladle can't request the soup,
a knife, the meat,
and so on.

We dip into lives where we're needed most and help trim away
the gristled parts.

I understand it better now; how mothers and fathers get this way.

The weekday drinking,

the crumpled mound of tobacco cartons collecting
in the rubbish bin,

the two a.m. tears that find their way to the second floor—
proof that we all end up the same,

and I understand it now.

Grandad was a steel-stock man,

    six-five on a hard day with hands like a bear;

        called him 'paw,' not because he was a grand,

but because he could palm a grown man's head like a basketball and pick him off the ground.

My 'pa' was a good one, steel-stock with hands like a bear.

Slap it on my Gumtree gravestone when I'm gone,

    a seven-word send-off that signifies the life I've led:

        "shot for the moon, hit the stars."

Scratch it deep with the pointed end of good intent to let the scions of my stead know my story—a half sonnet eulogy to tell of me.

Monday in a melancholy monsoon,

it was Earl Grey and overcoats as we perused Parisian thoroughfares.

Your insistence on lopsiding your mother's heirloom newsie cap made me laugh a little, but that sidelong glare told me tomorrow's torrential Tuesday would set a record.

Keeled over from left-arm pain on a mid-May Thursday once and went to heaven; found out it wasn't for me and caught a Greyhound back through the galaxy.

Wrote a letter to God when I got back and thanked the gang for their hospitality, but I just wasn't ready for forever.

That must've been the moment I knew;

the two of us cowering from the California sun in the shadow of your grandfather's avocado tree,

the way it was dying from age, the way we weren't.

That must've been the moment,
and I hold the thought of it back like a dry tear now.

Who am I within this algorithm ocean?

This sweeping expanse of expressionists
and aficionados of written word.

What more than a wayward vessel on syntax seas
of ones and zeros?

Than an ordinary oarsman,

rhythmless in his rowing,

stuck in whirlpools of his own inadequacy.

Good as it's been to me,

sedentary as a state of being's got these pesky old ramble-prone bones feeling unsettled.

There's more to see than the static and stand by placeholders of late-night television,

and my ficus feet are fixing to uproot and soil down somewhere else.

We're told what doesn't kill us makes us stronger.

But what of the little things that wear us down?

Do we ever speak to that?

To routine and dead-end drudgery,

the constant concern of checking accounts—things.

God help me, it's the day-to-day that gets the better of me.

A thing we should have said or done—that'd do it; would've, rather.

Pretenses in the past tense can't make up for the present,

                however,

                              and semantics were never my strong suit.

Writing wrongs
and piecing pain into patchwork quilted poetry
has always been my preference.

Just as well,
I suppose,
have a sit down with seventeen

and bum a smoke off my arrogance one more time before eighteen
and the last honest conversation I'll ever have.

Time and great tunes in the right tempo ease your grief eventually
and allow you to miss the people you hate most.

I am the poet's bane,

the folly of things forgotten

that rises from the dead to discharge through the felt lining
of your midnight pen.

I am the haunting that hardens the heart and calcifies the cartilage.

I am the sleepless nights and constant chasing—the poet's bane.

Flakes of February still flutter like filmstrips when I'm falling for someone else, and I wonder about forgiveness in courting another's smile.

You wonder if I wonder about anything;

little things, like tannins of Merlot grapes.

For February's sake, yes, I still wonder.

"That'll do," they'll say—my people, peers, and lovers spurned; when the curtains come down on this little anecdote of mine.

When cutaways to credit scenes and the cueing of a swan song send-off fall over my sunset silhouette,
    "that'll do," they'll say, exiting quietly.

Sundays are for sheet retreats and salvaging our sanity—
little breakaways from banalities beneath the bedding.

Sundays are for exaggerating how much sleep we should get and encouraging our electrons in the early hours.

It's for slow circling our sensuality like sharks.

I've come from nothing and chose to keep it that way.

The finer things never tickled my fancy, and I prefer minimalism to a mink coat.

Accouter me in shades of sequoia and campfire scent to connect me to my Mother, I'm of Her dust and dirt womb,

and hence I shall return.

Something insipid to muse my words today.

Anything other than the insufferability of old photo albums and grieving the greenhorn days gone by;

than the mulling of meaning and hesitations about my humanity.

Anything,

over the inundation of emotion,

to muse my words today.

Well, it's love again;

the kerf of a song lyric did it,
cut through the air like a band leader's baton,

and now I'm smitten.

Maybe it was the magnetism in their 4/4 measure
or the polarization of their pop melody personality,

but it's love again,
and a song lyric did it.

And for my final performance: atonement—
a recompense of my mortal defects.

How many times I've begrudged the beggarly hand
of my brothers and sisters.

How many times I've inclined my rapier wit like a sword unsheathed
against the pale and downtrodden.

And so,

I atone.

Midnight at a stoplight, and it's you again.

Story of my life,
middle of nowhere,
resting on red,
dwelling on a dimple,

fussing the little things—
palming an open hand and playful promiscuity.

Midnight at a stoplight,
and I'm waiting on a green to go on with my life.

Couldn't crumb a cracker on the kitchen counter without her knowing;

mother was keen like that, kept things clean,

called her a 'hawkeye' if you know what I mean.

Breakneck with a broomstick and Hell with a hand towel;

we never knew squalor—mother was keen like that.

Sure as sheets of storm clouds adieu,
I knew that day we'd sting like hail.

It's been longer now than you were then,
and something about that startles the strands of silver on my scalp.

Funny how we're nothing more than exercises in the abstract—
poems with no name or purpose.

Two a.m., and we're tappin' our toes, tootin' each other's horns and making a kind of music the neighbors might not approve of.

You're the tenor to my trombone tremolo,
and I'm a howlin' hound dog to your walking bass line.

It's jazz central,
       a swinging good time—sensual.

A thousand poems in your name,
and tonight a thousand more simply because I can't sleep.

Witchcraft and chamomile couldn't curb this ceaseless craving,

this unfounded fixation I have for all things algophilia—
the irony of painful pursuits in earning your praise.

Downtown,
and the shift of bodies drifting between shapeless strangers.

Where condensation quavers and curls up from the city's core,
and neon byways glimmer.

Downtown,
where humming 'crete and silence roar, where sequined minis shimmer.

Downtown.
    Our town.
        Yours.
            Mine.

I'll not my demons past efface;
I quite enjoy them in their place.

Of toilsome murk in midnight's fog,
we've weather-stayed abasement's bog.

Muddle-trudged capacious scale,
God's bountied-boon by some avail.

My demons, past by measures full,
have fortified my heart and soul.

How amusing, the misfortune of a suitor'd rose—
fascination of the foolhardy and allurement of the olfactory.

How senseless,

the blush of burgundy petals to incense our incessantly obsessive
sensibilities with stock and stem of salient ends to smart one's hands.

Boardwalk talk and the idyll air of a seagull breeze;

that one summer on the 'Cisco pier taught us all we'd ever need to know about being alive.

About being in love and the moon's mood swing temperament over the tides.

Time and again, I come to,

different me,

eternal you.

You'll come across yourself in the fog of a poem unknown someday and speculate the significance of page numbers,

calling on a quid pro quo to clarify your query;

I'll cheekily quip a stringent policy of never penning a kiss and telling of it—a knowing smile on my lips.

We'll be older then;

I'll be older, you'll be the very definition of a handled paperback, dog-eared and pocket-worn.

By and by,

steadily as the dissipation of audience applause,

a moment of conciliatory kinship will come between us—a state of ubiquity that settles down.

Took a drive on Highway 40 recently to relive life at #59—a teaming trailer park community in my youth dried up and deserted as a tumbleweed tract now.

Caught the smart end of a xyloid broom there once for not latching the back door; I think on that as I strike a match.

I'd sought you as your summer name, a pseudonym by which you'd aired poetic grievances.

Our time together was an adventure in Twain:

spirited,

remarkable,

and rife with danger.

But autumn'd asked too much, it seems,
and all good things must end as dreams—recurrent misery.

Speak us a setback in a Saturday night slam session,

somewhere in the crisp of coffee beans and single shots, take yours.

Teach the audience something they won't soon forget when you spit my name from your mouth;

express me as espresso burn—a tingle on your tongue.

Stumbled once,
        rather irreverently,

into the cultured lacuna of a buskers square,
situated just 'atween the hapless temperament of bowery slums
and the porcine obduracy of opulence.

The diction there was solely digraphical—
phonetic poetry thrumming with bohemian pathos.

Percussion winds and the steady melodies of reed movement by
wheedled banks where song thrush cup in tiresome nest to croon.

Slow, in the hushed sanction of sommer's ebb tide eve,
my feathered hands quietly quill the follies of my father—
my sainted mother's misfortunes.

The quarter moon could not have been more patient; lo these many months, the obeisant night sky stars withheld your name from their polished tongues.

And what say thee,

> o' patroness of trembling hands,
> of your earthly muse?

Aye, I, who wouldst thou wayward heart reform?

Some days, it's the simple things—
your kitchen counter countenance and the little death
that came before we did.

Some days,

it's the wind whispering your whereabouts or a hundred nameless
poems we swore to never speak aloud.

Some days, it's the little death that came of us.

Ashes to ashes, and so on and so forth;

Nineteen me knew it long before I ever had to—
the pain of atoning for those what can't be saved.

I called myself a Christian then,
but I won't speak the name now save in vain.

Nothing can prepare you for the weight of dust to dust.

Tonight I'll content to let history interpret the words—the layered obscurity I left in my stead.

I'll let the whos' and the whats' be determined by bearded and bookwormed philosophers,

by babes of the bard-hearted and bold,
scattered and stained forever on printed page.

Veranda sunrise with a cuppa somethin',

and not a soul in sight to sully the moment.

Here I hide,

sparrow carolers resounding their springsong love affair beneath the pull of my stable sip—slow,

so as to stay off the sound of slurp,

steadfast to stimulate my morning senses.

A cavalcade of questions, but how to carry on when you've seen too much?

I think on that,
a father now,

reflecting my own father bearing witness to a father crying his son's name in the Teton streets.

What to say to a man who became a man as a young boy?

                    I am unaware.

A firm twenty, and I still fidget weighing what I'd write;

what I'd say to the wide-eyed wonder living alone in the two-story on South Road in the small town I ran away from.

Funny thing,

the miles between us,

how they stretch and wind a firm twenty,

and still I fidget.

Tune that ol' gitbox down a step to the tempo of the steps down my
back stoop;
      to the fragrance of pine fir and flannel,
      the musk of my old man's rolled Marlboros,

and the cadence of a cracked cold one over a crackling fire—
fresh from the chill of river basket cool off.

Maybe there was more to say,

but maybe time and tepid bathwater got in the way—
or maybe that's just the last line in a lukewarm love affair.

Maybe hard rain had something to do with it,

how you described dead things in a downpour.

Maybe someday I'll say your name,

maybe.

Inundated again,

it's a fog wash of a Friday, and Saturday's shaping up to be sopping with sog and symptoms of cherophobia.

Someone's rainbow is coming in somewhere,

I speculate,

slipping into skin of melancholy melanin—were that I a fish, scales aglimmer as I swim away.

This one's for birds and sky,

for tumbled rocks and riverbeds.

For green things and growing old, for paper-penned love letters that were never sent,

and the ones that were. It's for sons and daughters who grow into mothers and fathers,

for music and musing—living, dying.

Cuticle crust,
and the daily doldrums of summer breeze scented detergent;

this is what looking back on a leap of faith chalks up to,
complimenting Kodachrome pictures of your youthful ignorance

and cursing the Polaroid printout
you're passing yourself off as these days.

A season,

for every season,

or so I'm told—a mood for the months of melancholia,

something stimulating for the sunshine spell and an atmosphere of introspection in autumn's rueful resplendence.

I think on that as I regard the vacillant nature of retreating follicles.

You,

    who will inherit my demons,
     my high brow, and brittle bones.

You,

    who will fashion and wear your soul a cape of anger as I did;
    who will fisticuff the whole of creation to know your father's heart.

You,

    whose shadow will overshadow someone else's with time.

Acknowledgments

To my family, friends, and amazing followers, I must express eternal gratitude. Your tireless support lifts my spirits daily and continues to give me strength and inspiration in my endeavors and writing. I truly could not chase my dreams without your love. If my words have reached you in any way, please, kindly leave a review for this book. Your time and thoughts are important to me.

About the Author

A lover of words and the impact they create, Ty Gardner is a lifelong enthusiast of all forms of poetry and has written creatively from the time he was a child.

When he's not musing and waxing poetic, Ty can be found exploring the wonderment of his newfound home in Northwest Arkansas with his wife, two children, and their handsome rescue pup, Archer.

He is the author of *By Way of Words: A Micro Prose Journey Through the Elements That Mold Us*, *Bukowski Charm: Trash Fire Poetry to Warm the Soul*, *Wild Life: Musings of a Mad Poet*, *From the Watercolor Garden: Poems of Life and Love*, *A Thousand Little Things: One-line Poems to Spark a Thought*, *Sunsets Over Cityscapes: Poems for the Existential Uprising*, *Papercut: A Chap-style Book of Prose*, and *Average American: Poems On Becoming Normal*. Some of his works can also be found in *VSS365 Anthology: Volume One*, released in September 2019.

Printed in Great Britain
by Amazon